PIANO SOLO

DAVID LANZ

east of the moon

www.davidlanz.com

Management:
W.F. Leopold Management
4425 Riverside Drive, Suite #102
Burbank, CA 91505

ISBN 0-634-01102-2

HAL•LEONARD®
CORPORATION

7777 W. BLUEMOUND RD. P.O. BOX 13819 MILWAUKEE, WI 53213

For all works contained herein:
Unauthorized copying, arranging, adapting, recording or public performance is an infringement of copyright.
Infringers are liable under the law.

Visit Hal Leonard Online at
www.halleonard.com

Composer's note: Some of the orchestral parts from the CD have been added to these piano transcriptions. They may be omitted if so desired.

THE GREEN MAN

By DAVID LANZ

Moderately fast, in 2

* Optional orchestral introduction. Solo piano version begins on page 6.

Copyright © 2000 by Moon Boy Music (BMI)
All Rights Reserved   Used by Permission

(uilleann pipe)

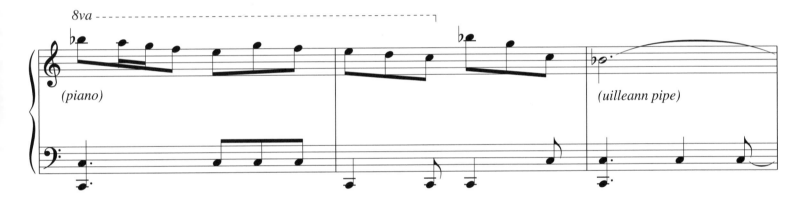

(piano)

(uilleann pipe)

6

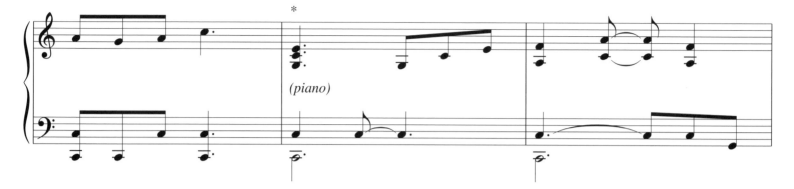

(piano)

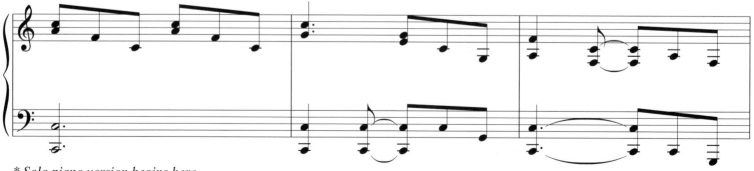

* Solo piano version begins here.

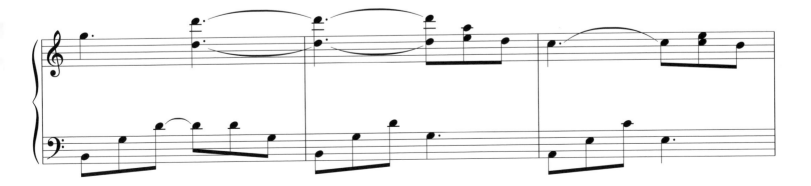

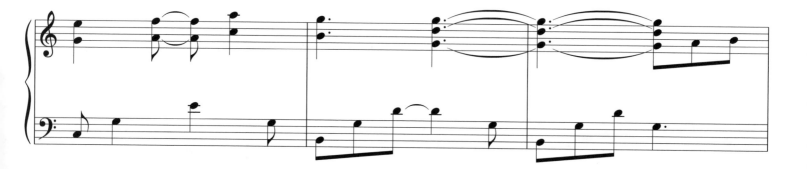

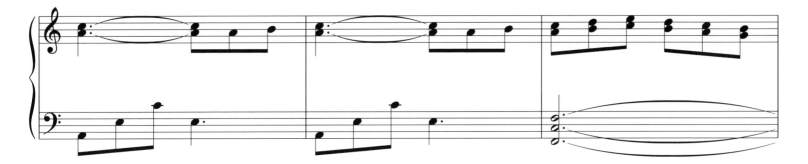

To Coda ⊕

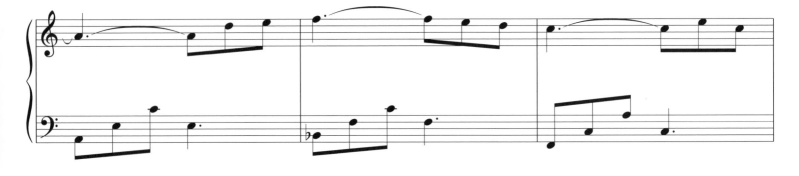

D.S. al Coda

CODA

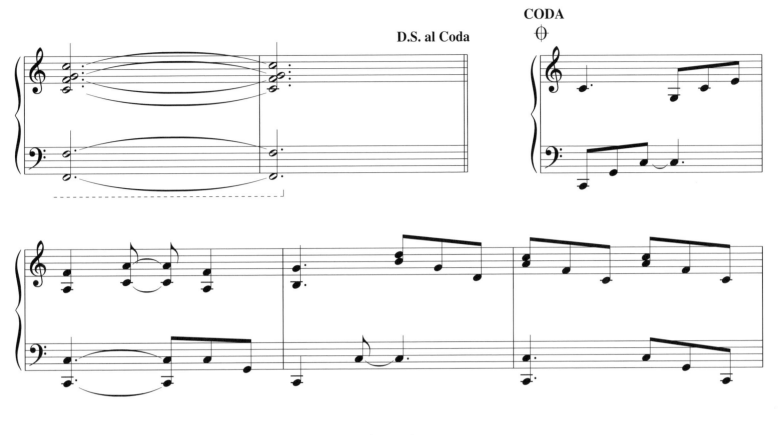

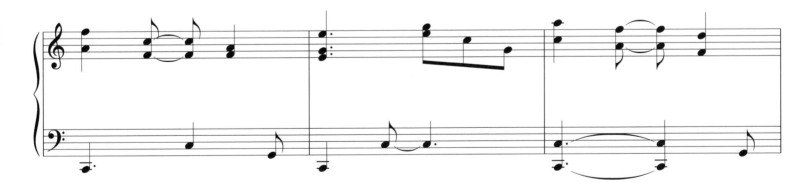

12

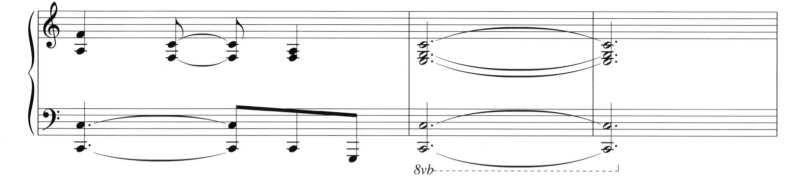

8vb- -

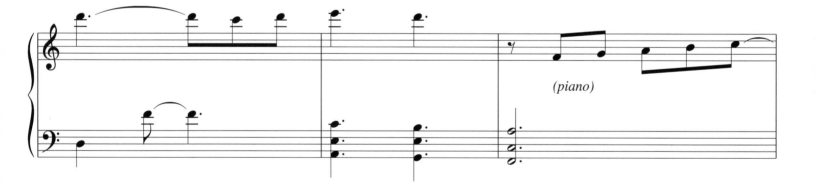

mp   (flute)

(piano)

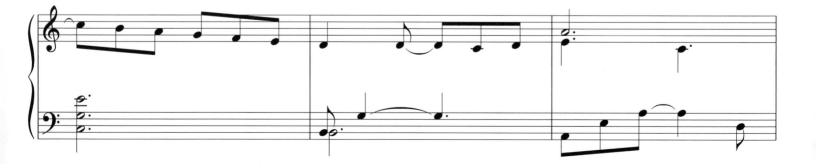

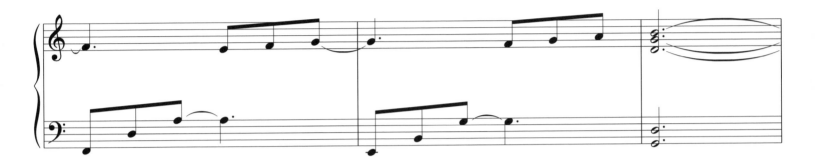

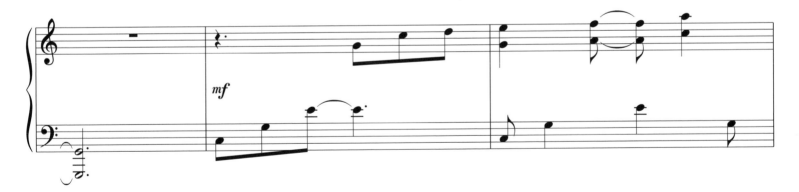

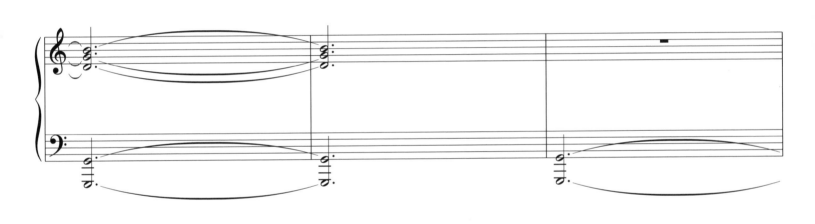

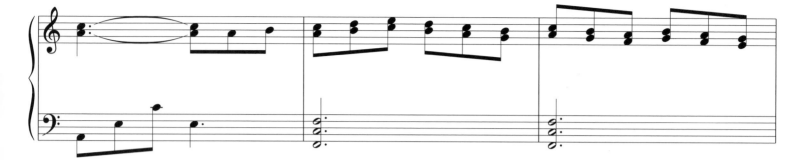

1.,2.　　　　　　　　　　　　　　　3.

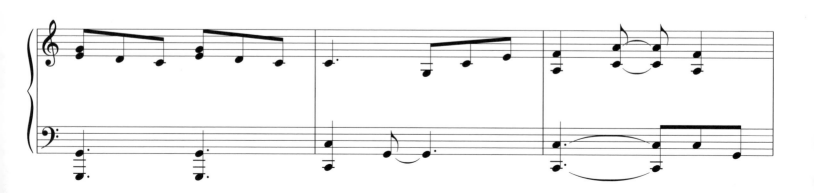

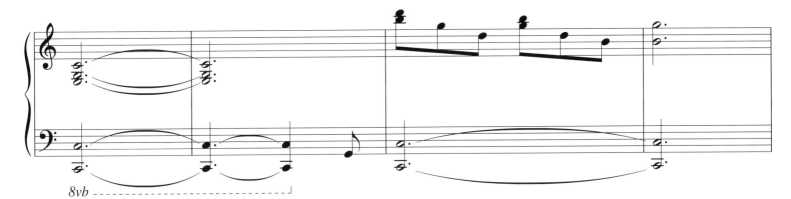

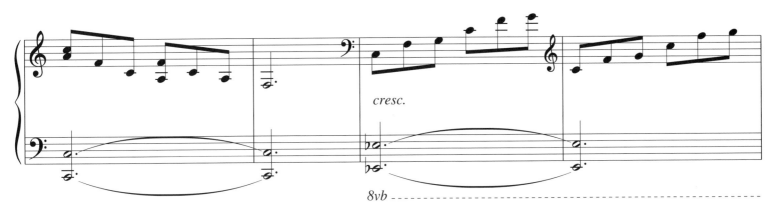

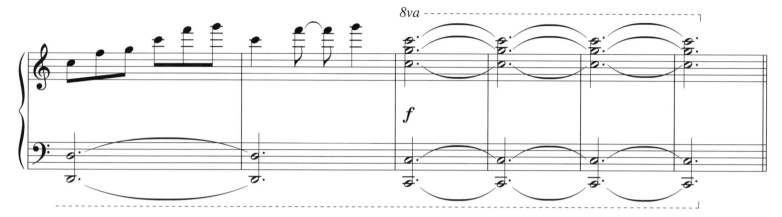

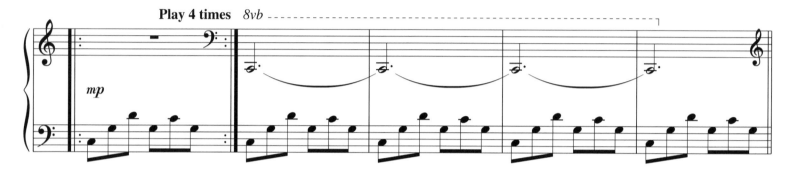

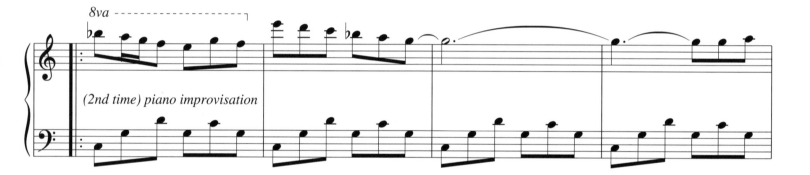

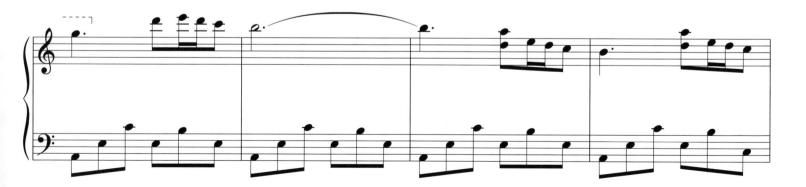

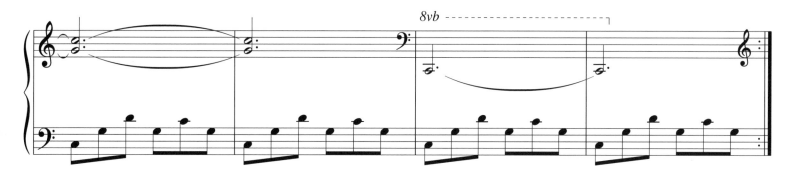

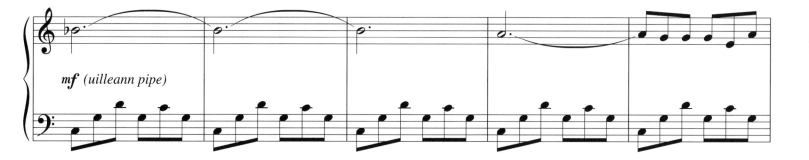

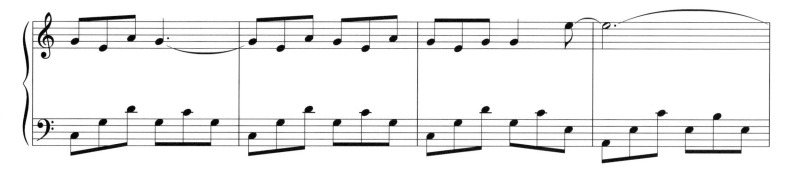

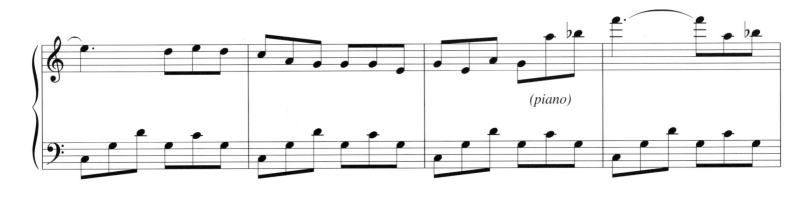

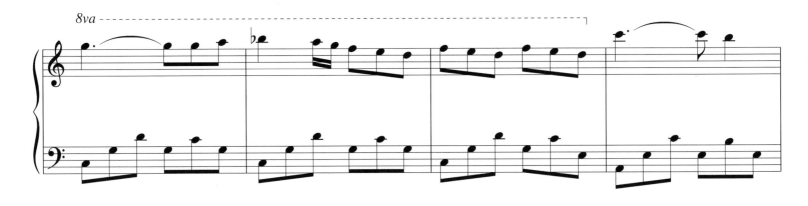

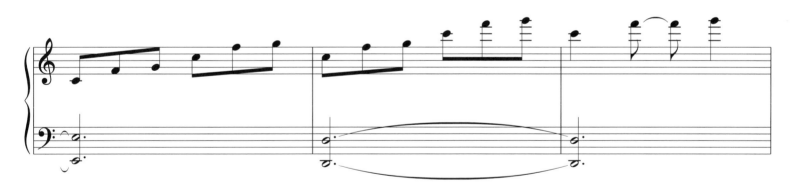

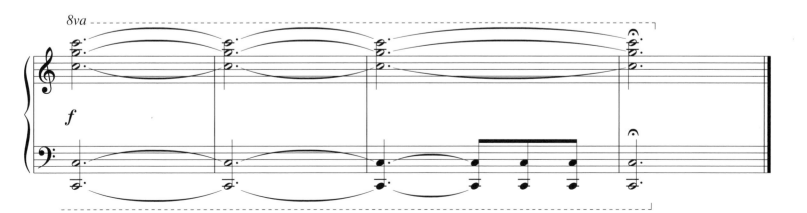

DANCING WITH DIONYSOS

By DAVID LANZ

Moderately fast

Copyright © 2000 by Moon Boy Music (BMI)
All Rights Reserved   Used by Permission

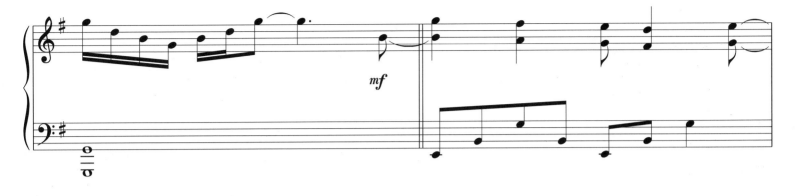

22

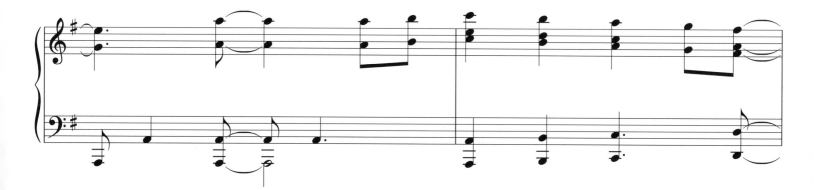

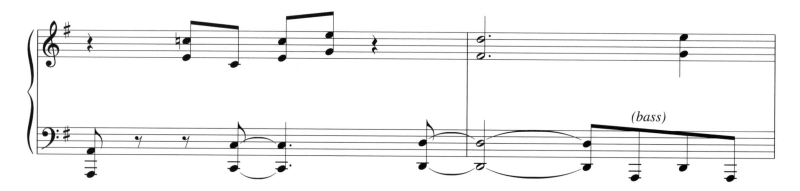

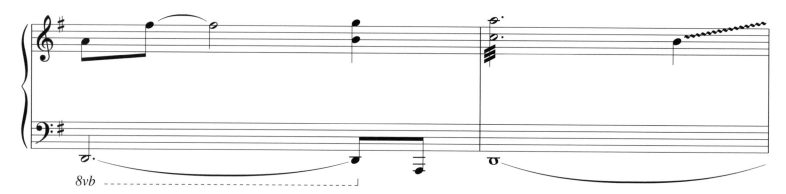

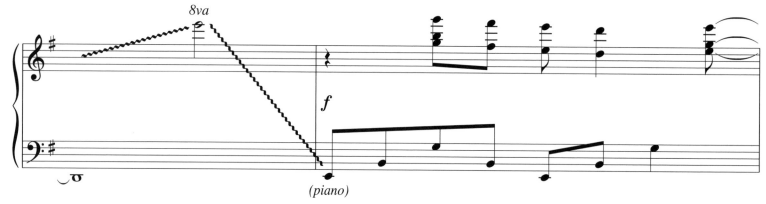

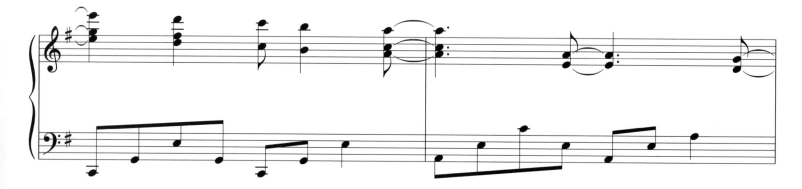

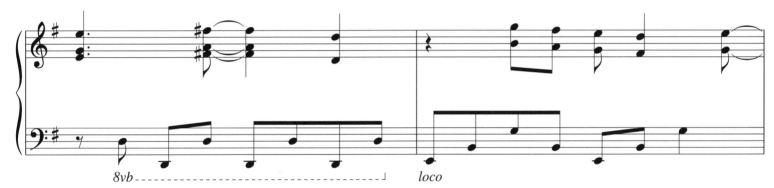

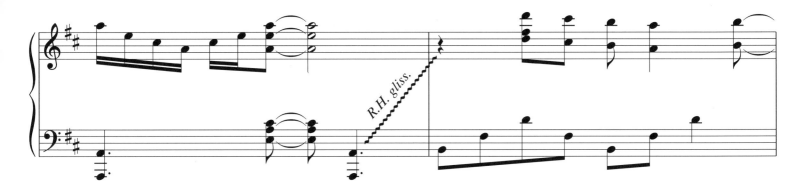

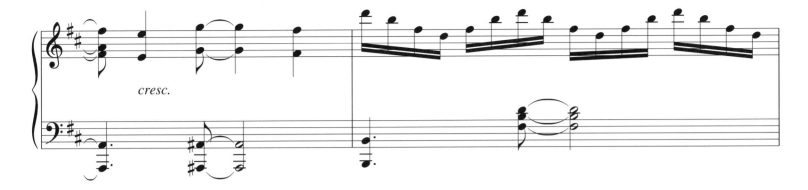

cresc.

8vb

8vb

8vb

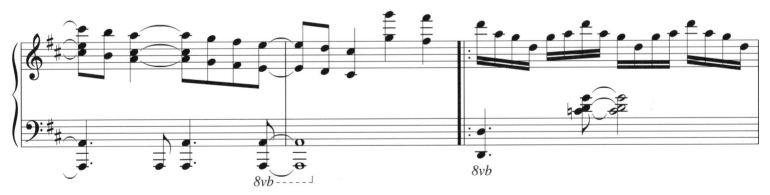

8vb

8vb

Repeat and Fade | **Optional Ending**

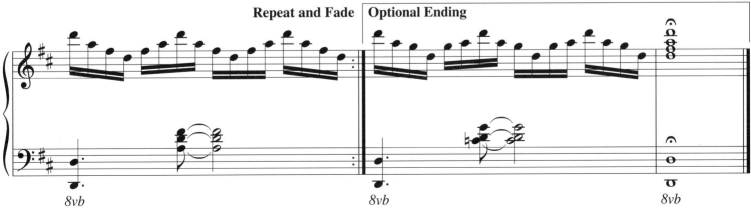

8vb

8vb

8vb

CHASING APHRODITE

By DAVID LANZ

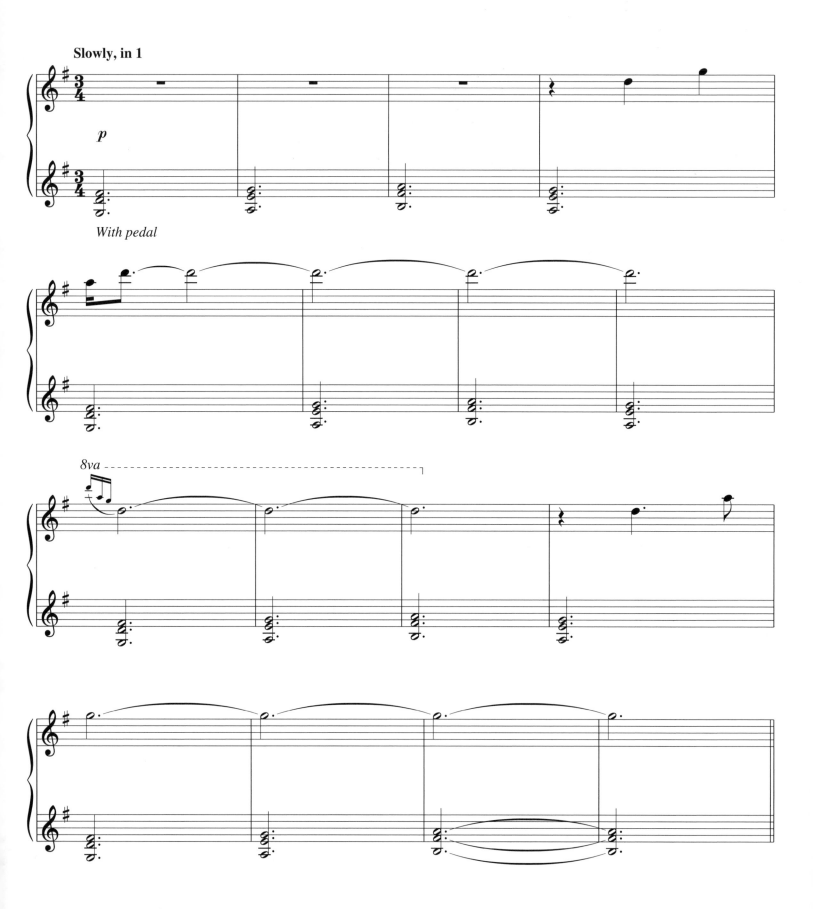

Copyright © 2000 by Moon Boy Music (BMI)
All Rights Reserved   Used by Permission

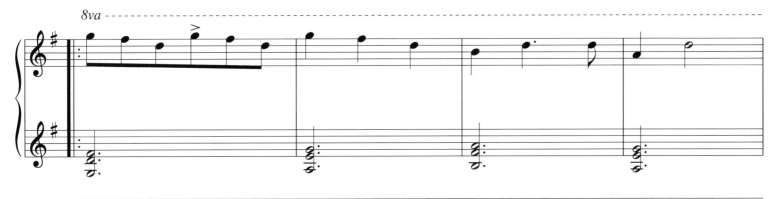

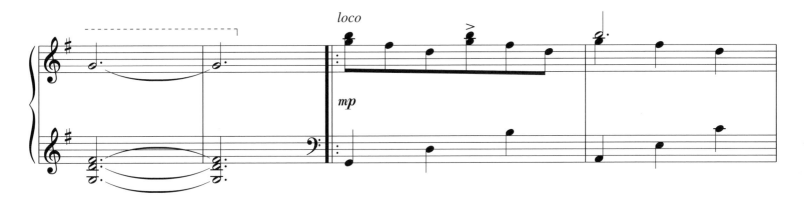

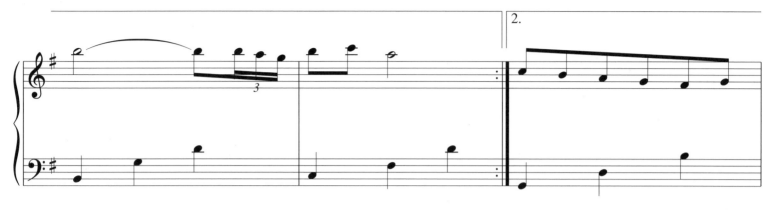

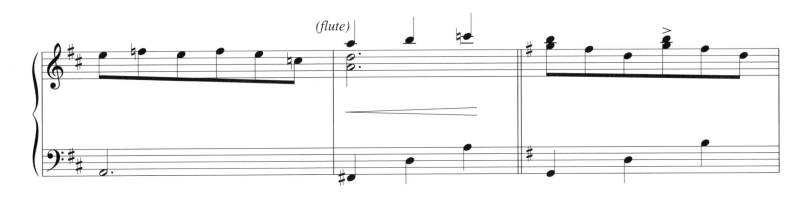

To Coda $\oplus$

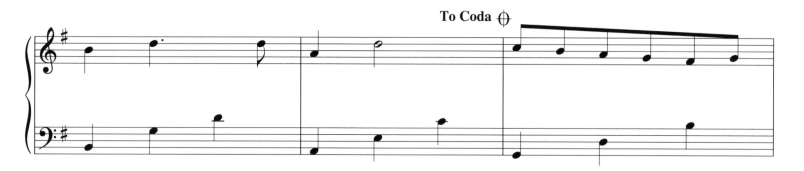

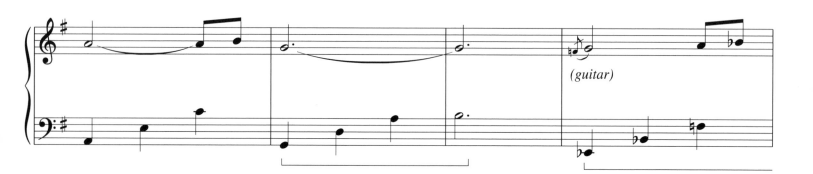

(guitar)

(piano)

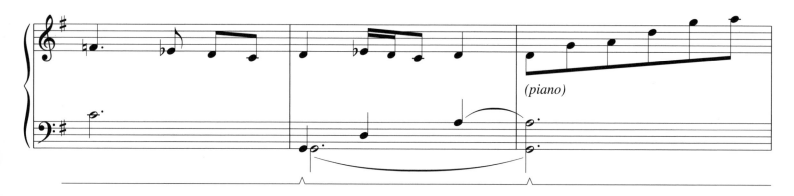

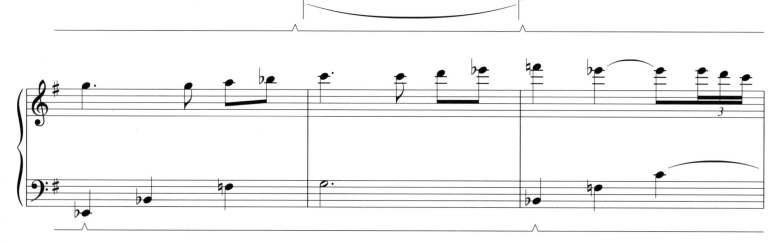

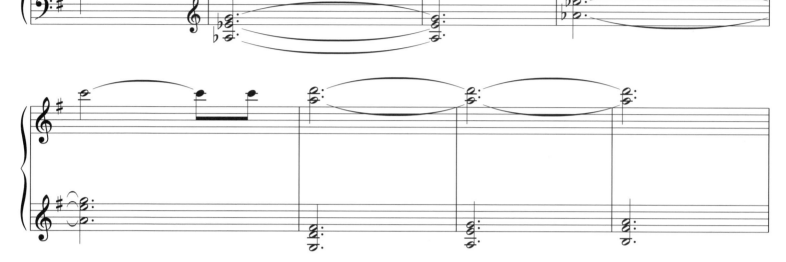

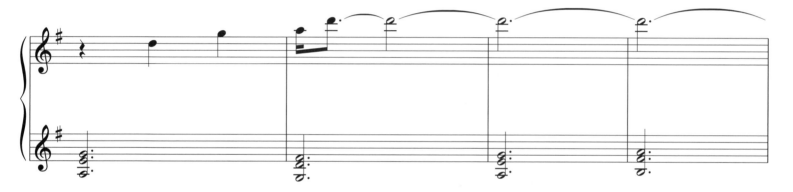

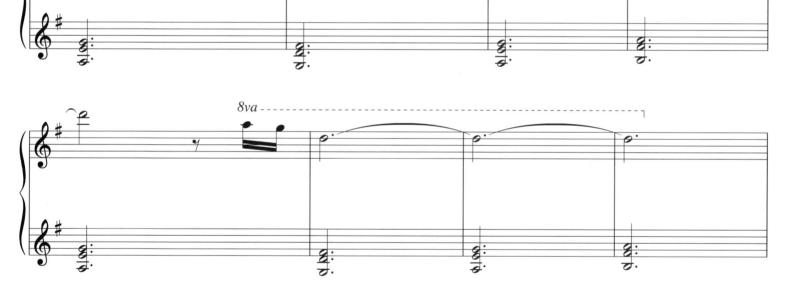

D.S. al Coda

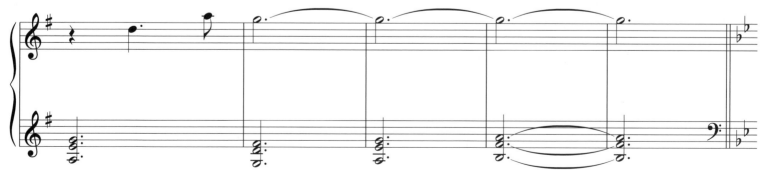

CODA

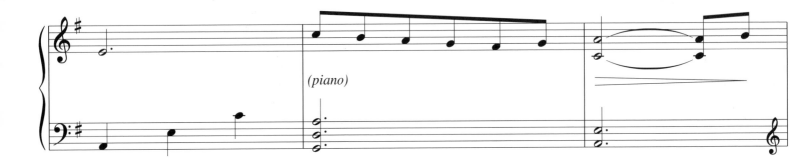

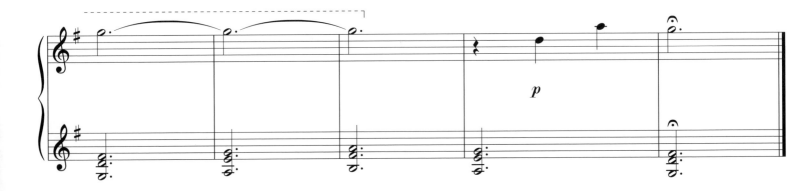

EAST OF THE MOON

By DAVID LANZ

Copyright © 2000 by Moon Boy Music (BMI)
All Rights Reserved   Used by Permission

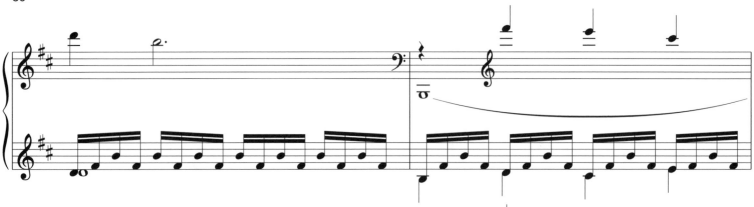

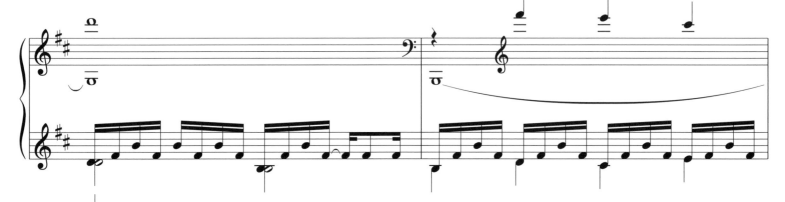

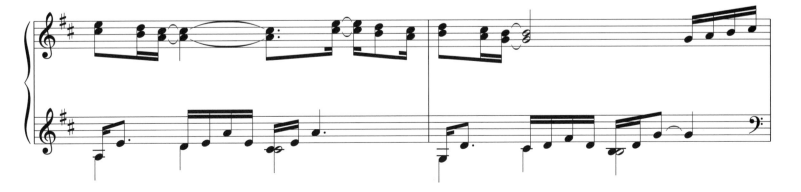

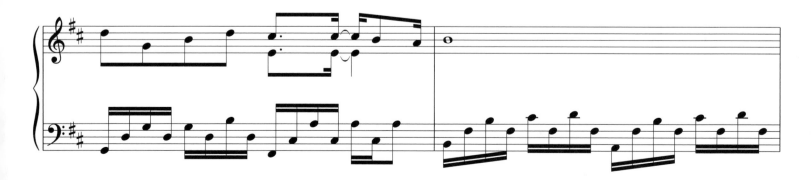

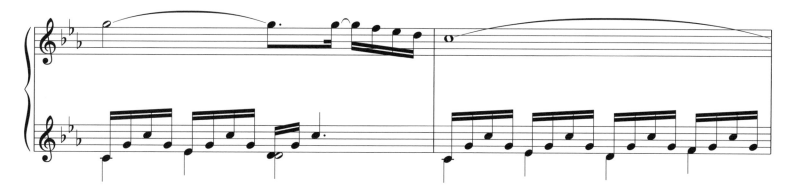

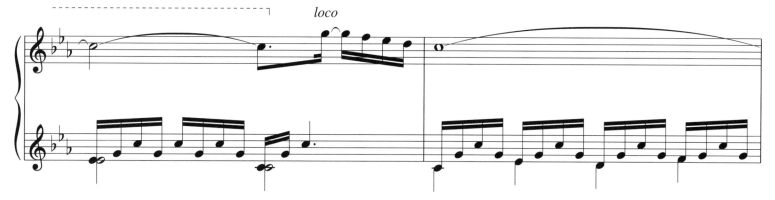

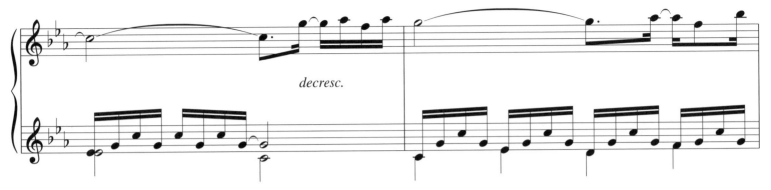

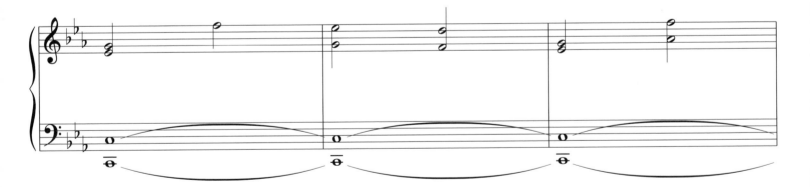

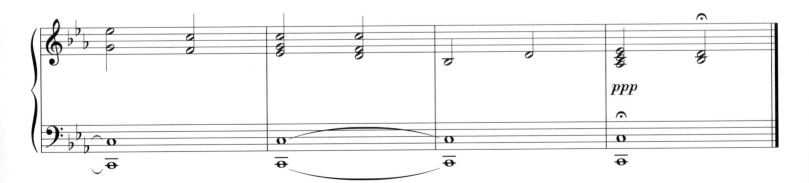

ON THE EDGE OF A DREAM

By DAVID LANZ

Copyright © 2000 by Moon Boy Music (BMI)
All Rights Reserved   Used by Permission

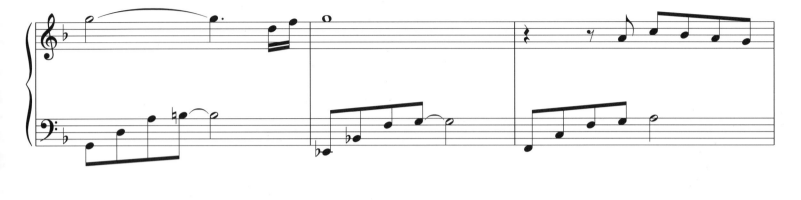

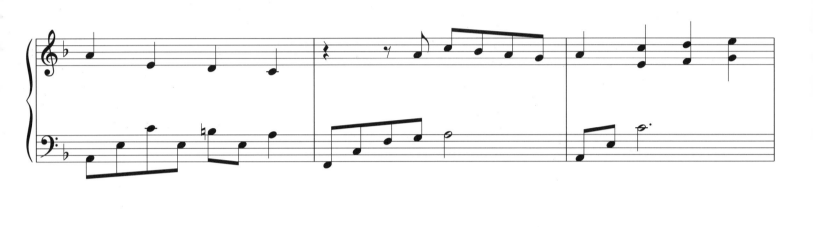

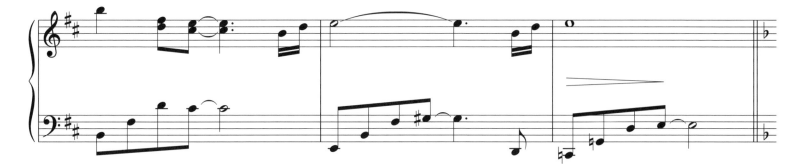

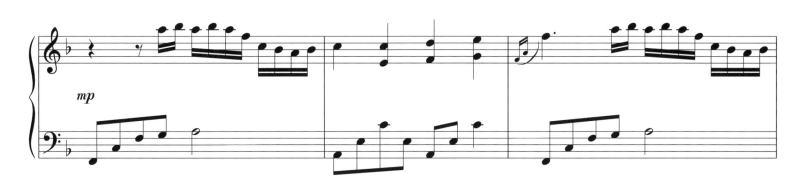

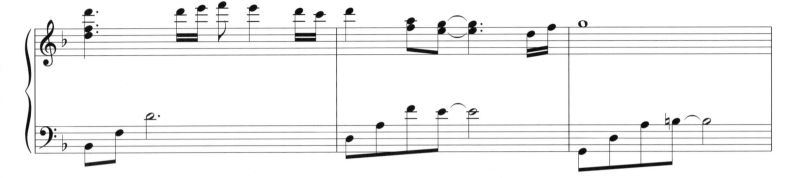

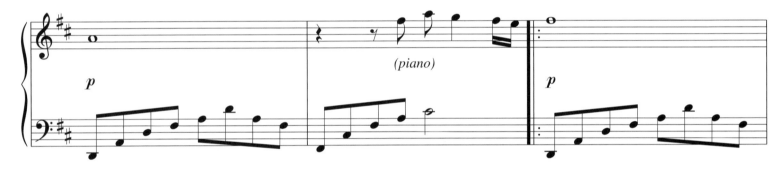

Repeat and Fade

Optional Ending

Slower

rit.

AND TIME STOOD STILL

By DAVID LANZ

Moderately slow

Copyright © 2000 by Moon Boy Music (BMI)
All Rights Reserved   Used by Permission

(synthesizer countermelody)

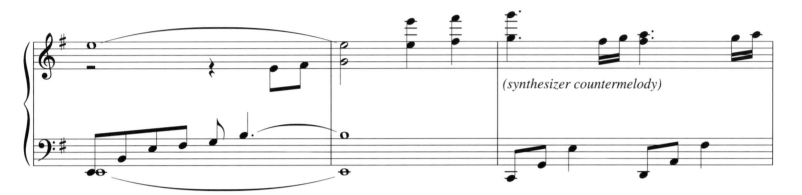

3

(strings)

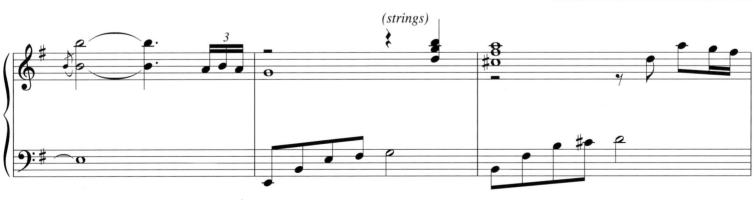

3

(piano and guitar)
mf

cresc.

(piano)

8vb

mf

(organ countermelody)

8vb

3

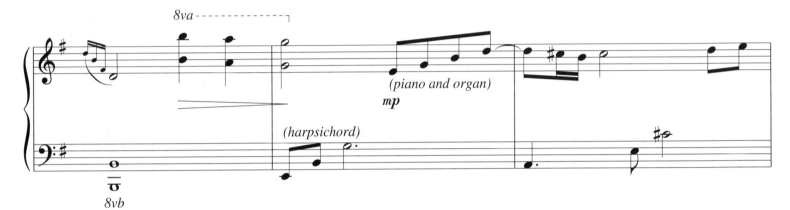

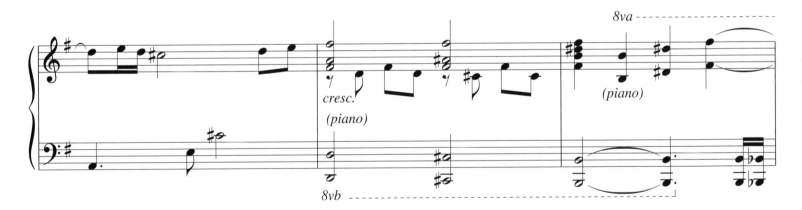

(string countermelody)

Repeat ad lib. and Fade

(organ)

(piano)

Optional Ending

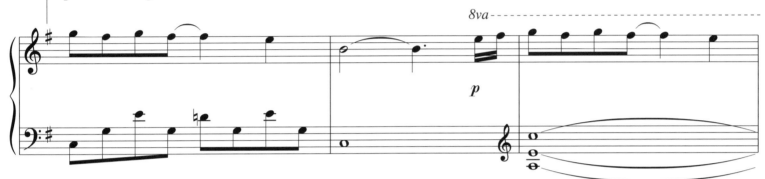

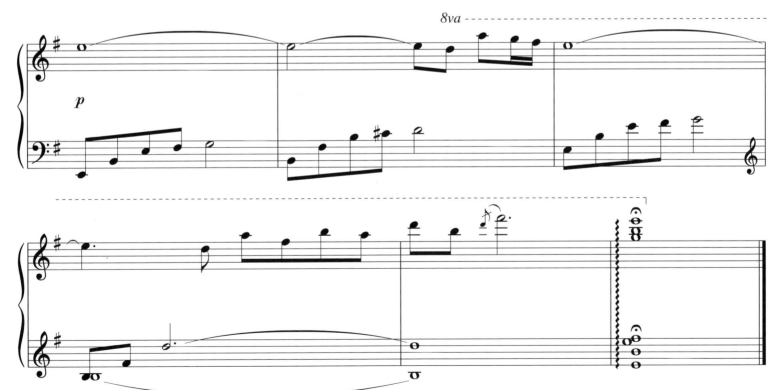

TARA

By DAVID LANZ

Slowly, in 2

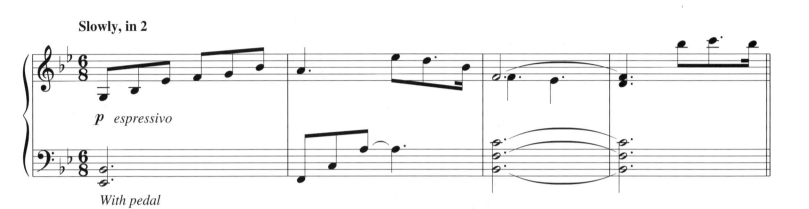

p espressivo

With pedal

cresc.

mp

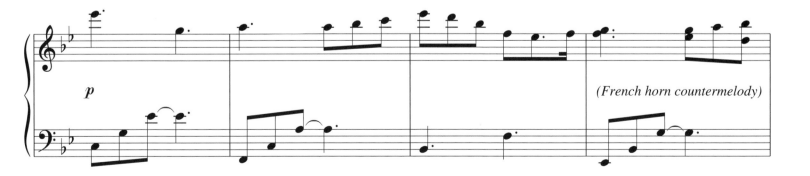

p

(French horn countermelody)

Copyright © 2000 by Moon Boy Music (BMI)
All Rights Reserved   Used by Permission

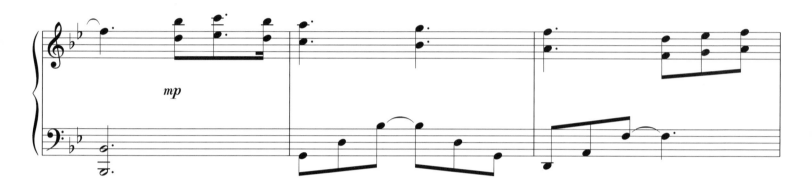

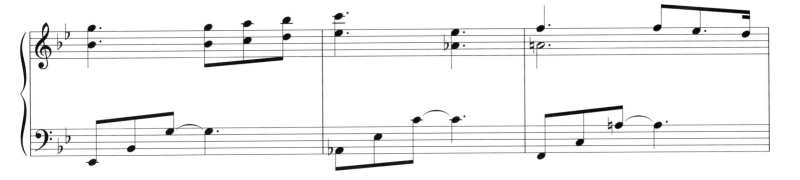

56

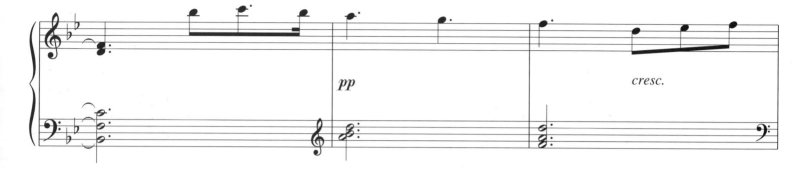

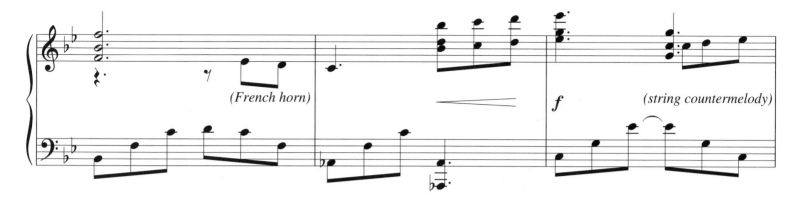

(French horn)

f

(string countermelody)

decresc.

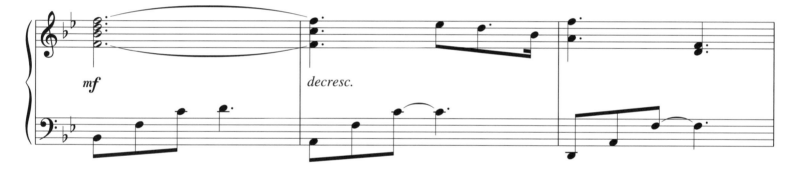

mf

decresc.

mp

rit.

Freely

WORLD AT PEACE
(Music for Piano & Orchestra in Six Parts)

I. Declaration Overture

By DAVID LANZ

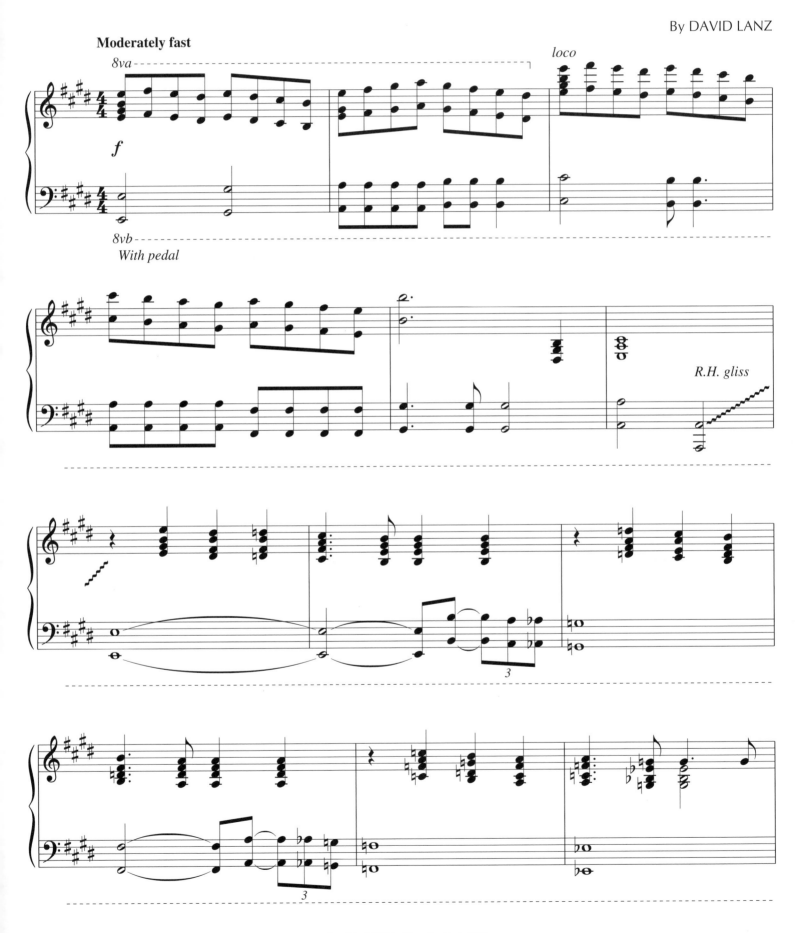

Copyright © 2000 by Moon Boy Music (BMI)
All Rights Reserved   Used by Permission

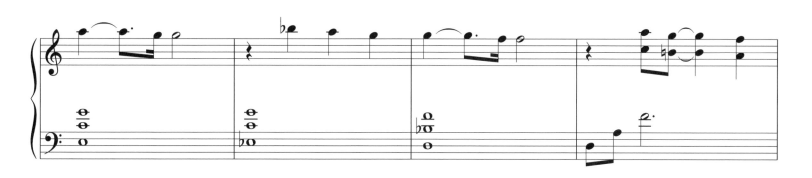

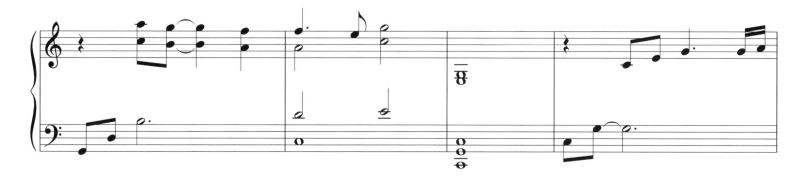

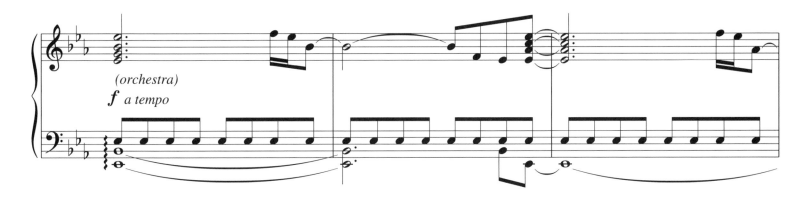

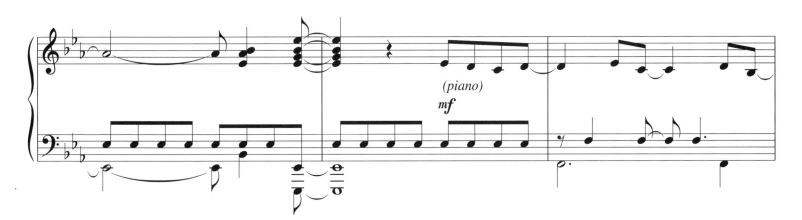

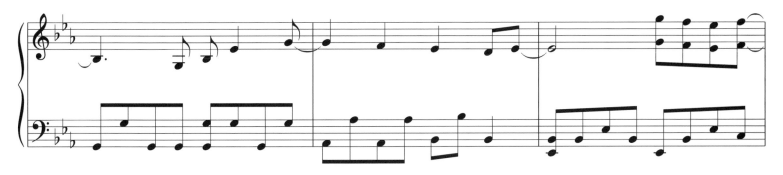

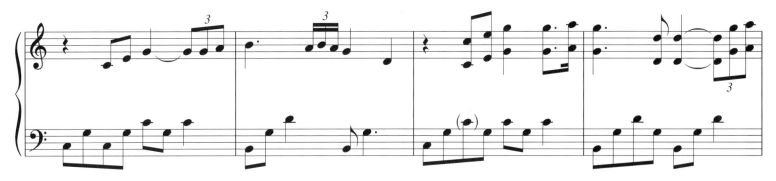

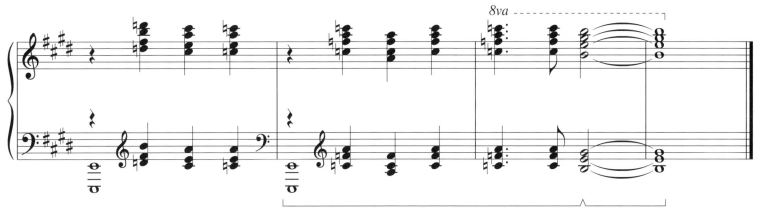

II. Prayer of Peace

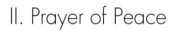

Solemnly

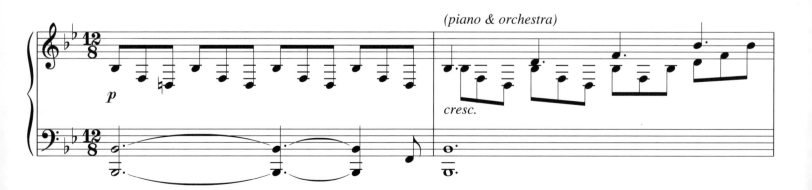

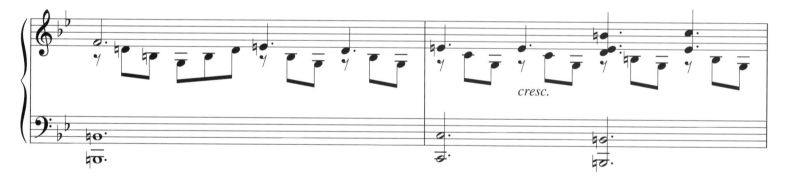

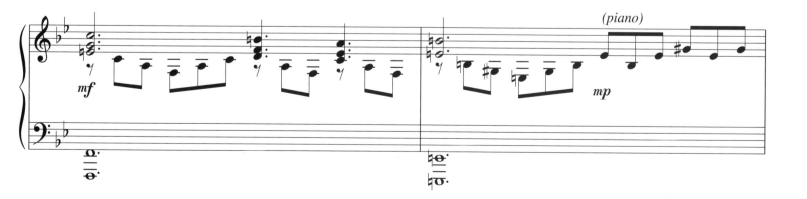

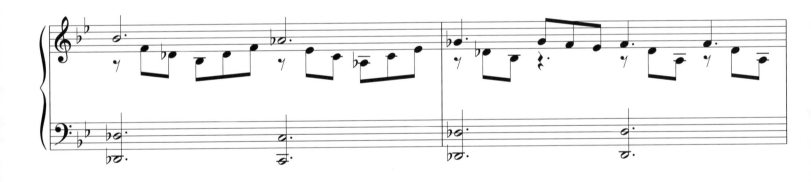

III. Gaia: Goddess Reborn

Moderately fast

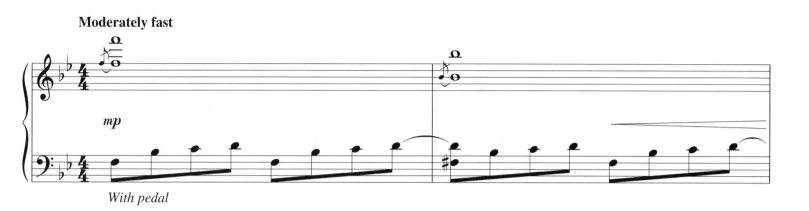

mp

With pedal

rit.   *a tempo*

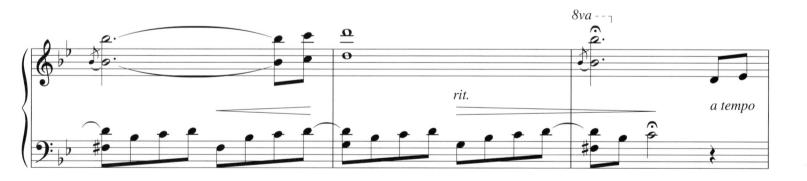

rit.   *a tempo*   *8va*

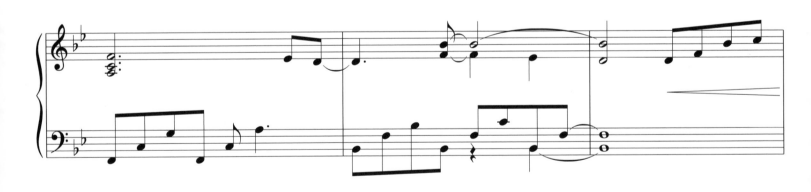

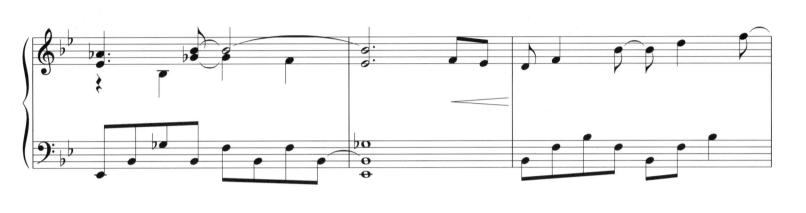

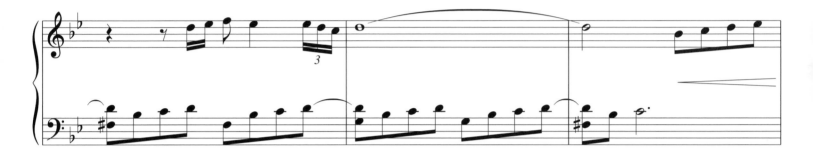

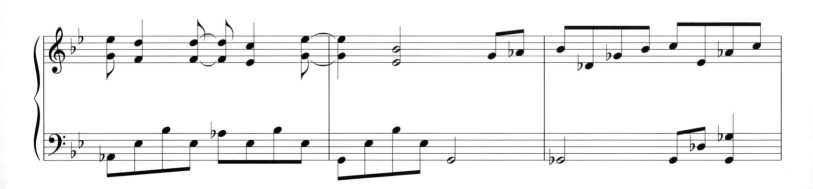

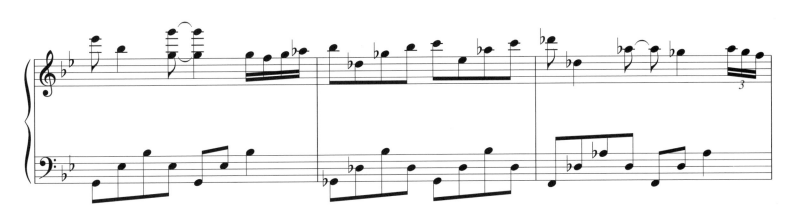

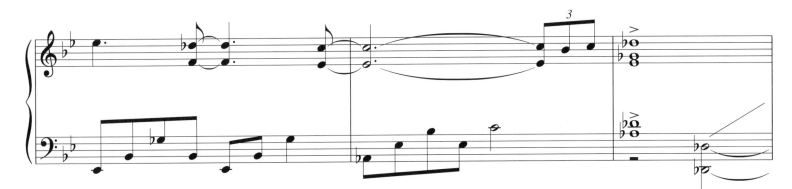

A little slower

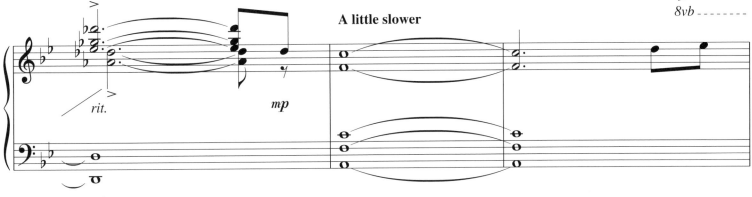

IV. New World Turning

Trimphantly

* The orchestral introduction is omitted from this arrangement.

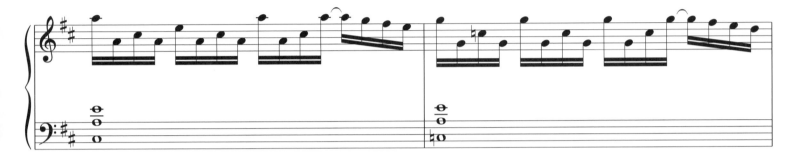

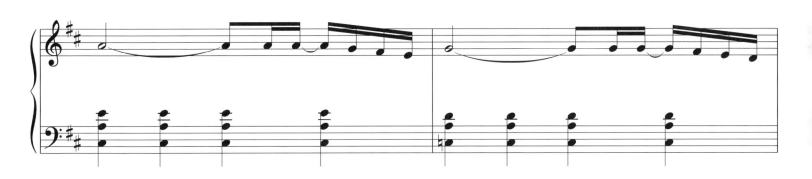

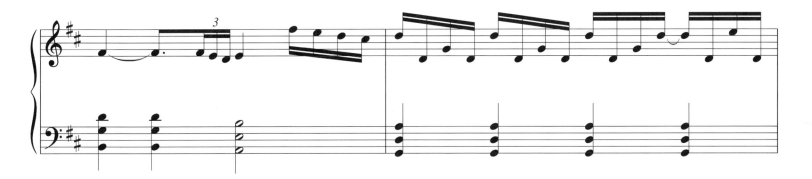

cresc.

D.C. al Coda

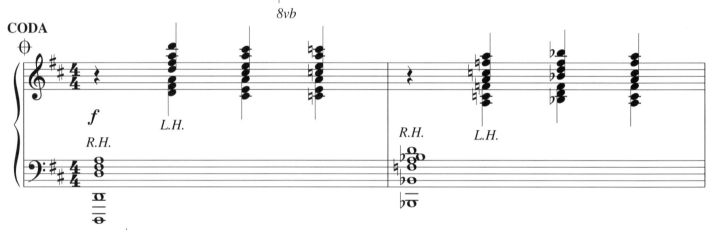

CODA

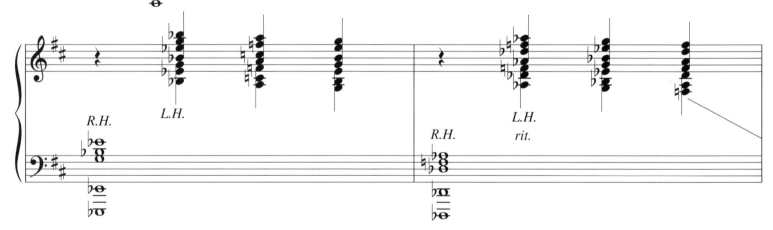

V. Renaissance

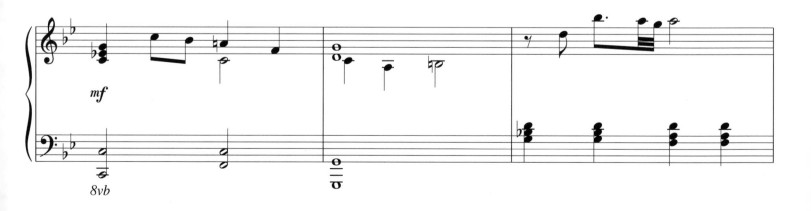

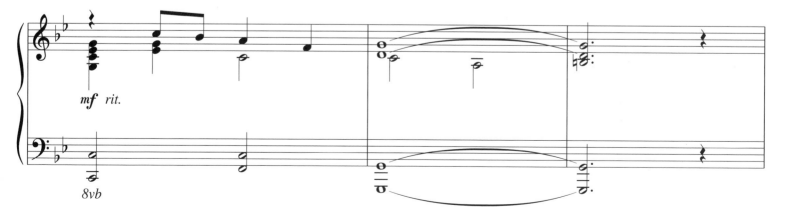

82

VI. Transformation

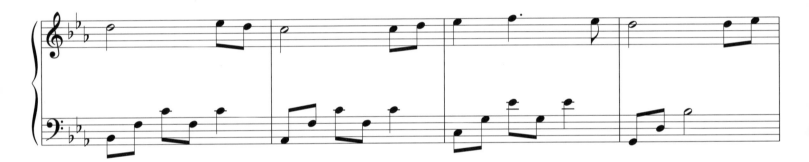

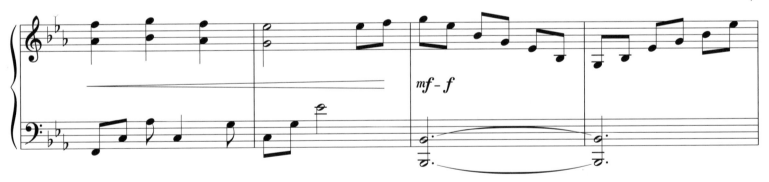

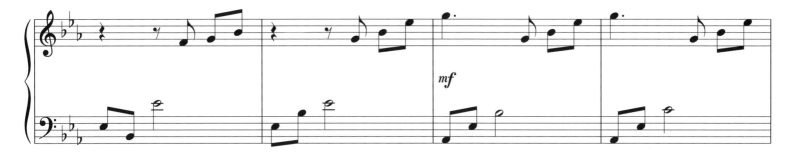

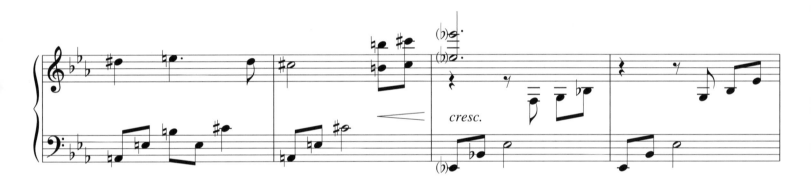

D.S. al Coda

CODA

A little faster

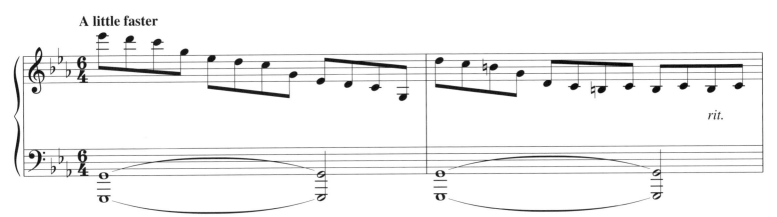

Moderately

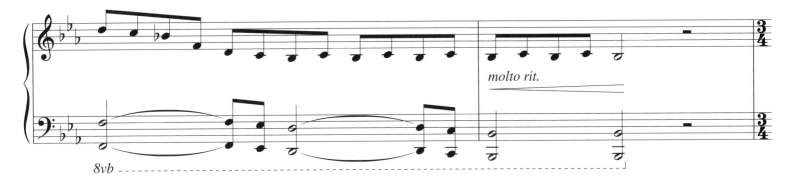

Moderately fast

Moderately

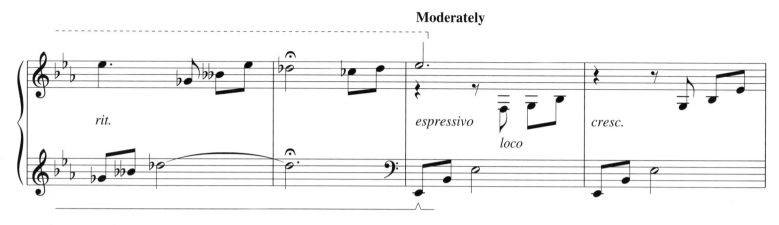

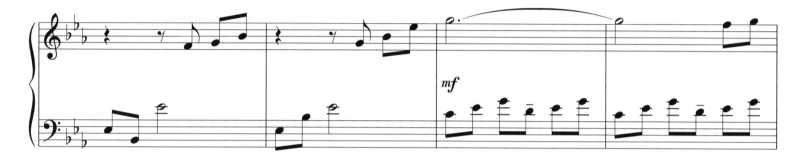

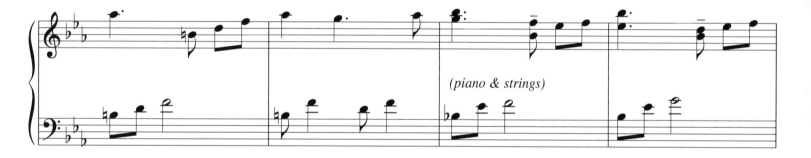

THE VISITOR

By DAVID LANZ

Slowly, with expression

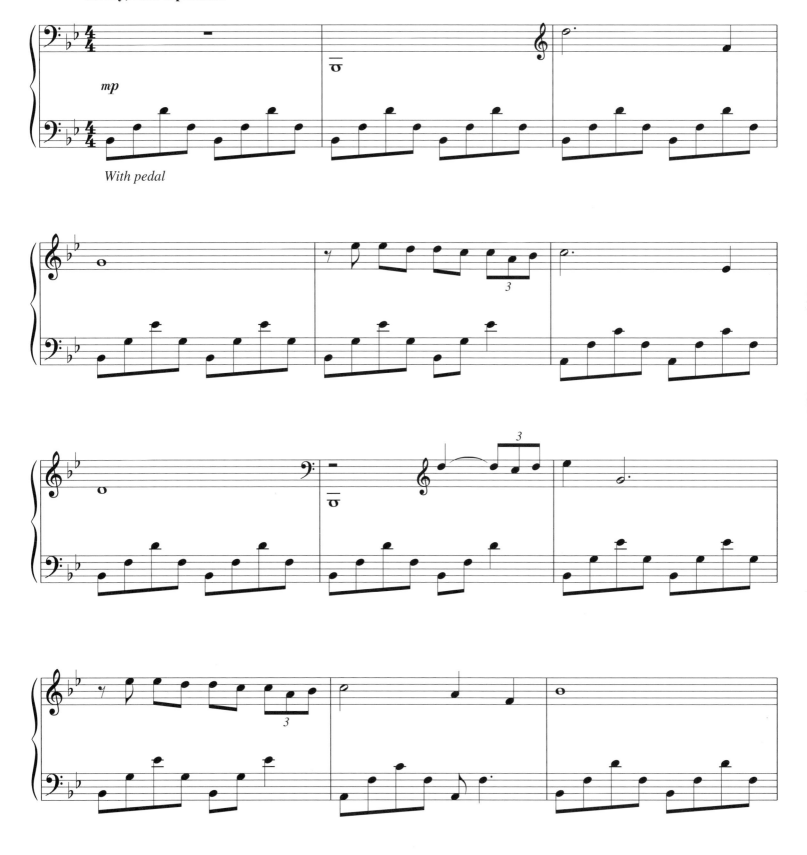

With pedal

Copyright © 2000 by Moon Boy Music (BMI)
All Rights Reserved   Used by Permission

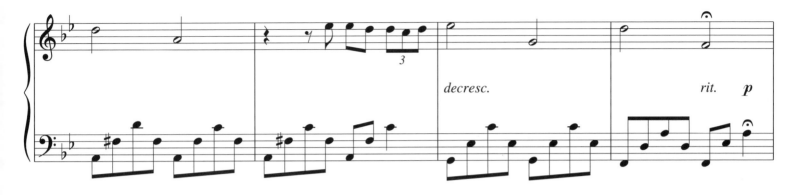

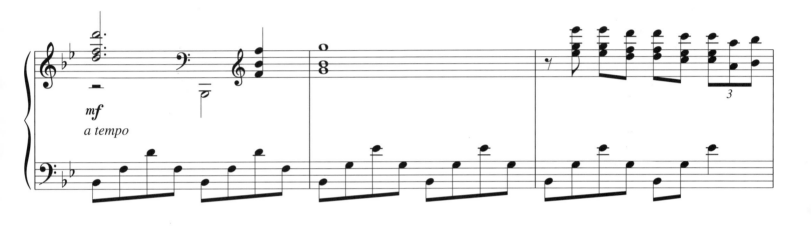

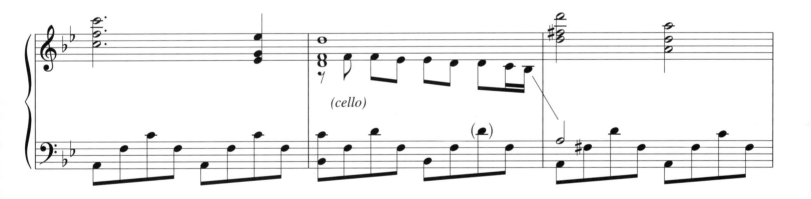

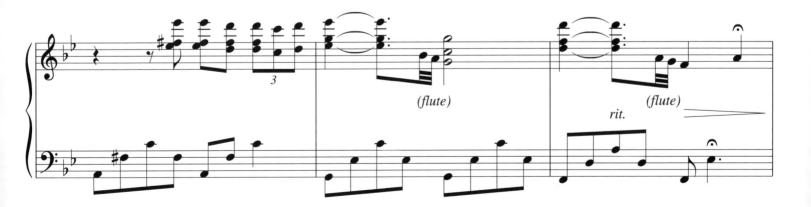

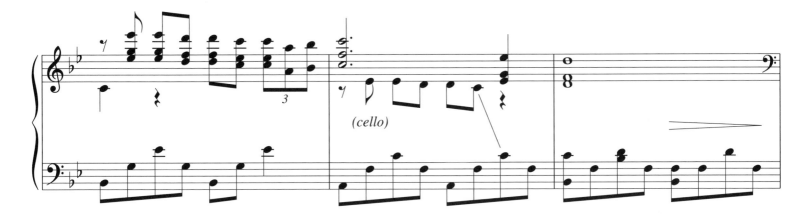

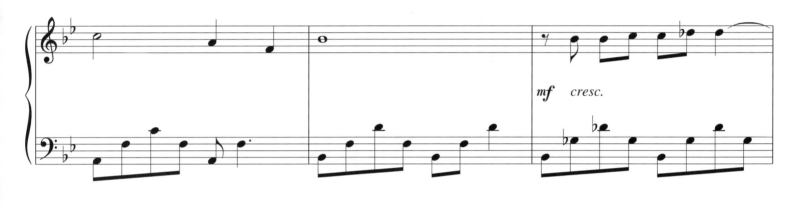